Cheap Thrills Cuisine®

with Chef Peppi

Chef Peppi

Cheap Thrills Cuisine®

with Chef Peppi

A Collection of Quick, Tasty, Creative Recipes

By Lombardo & Bùi

LB
1837

Little, Brown and Company
BOSTON NEW YORK TORONTO LONDON

First Edition

Library of Congress Cataloging-in-Publication Data

Lombardo, Bill.
Cheap thrills cuisine with Chef Peppi: a collection of quick, tasty, creative recipes/Bill Lombardo and Thach Bui.
p. cm.
Includes index.
ISBN 0-316-53092-1
1. Quick and easy cookery. 2. Comic books, strips, etc. I. Bui, Thach. II. Title.
TX833.5.L66 1995
641.5'55 — dc20 95-9813

10 9 8 7 6 5 4 3 2 1

HAD

Published simultaneously in Canada by Little, Brown & Company (Canada) Limited

Printed in the United States of America

Contents

Introduction

Welcome to CHEAP THRILLS CUISINE, a collection of no-fuss recipes in a comic strip format. With Chef Peppi as your guide, you are about to embark on a culinary journey through the world of international cuisine, without leaving your kitchen.

In the early 1970s, we lived next door to one another in Toronto. Our collaboration began when Bill was attending a culinary college in Toronto for advanced chef training, and Thach was working as a freelance cartoonist. The campus was located in Kensington Market, an enclave noted for international food shops, butchers, and fish markets. We'd meet for lunch and stroll the streets, turning over lobsters and sorting through clams, often ending up in an ethnic restaurant.

Thach would often watch Bill cook and instead of jotting down recipes would draw them. CHEAP THRILLS CUISINE was born from these thumbnail instructions.

As the oldest of six boys, Bill often helped his mother cook. She rarely worked from recipes. Bill

combines ingredients as she would, trying something new and interesting or adapting traditional dishes for the fast-paced needs of today. Our recipes incorporate humor and simplicity, while keeping an eye on classical technique.

Growing up in Vietnam, Thach was always fascinated by a nearby market, with food sellers stir-frying lemon grass and cardamom in the open air. He has enriched Bill's knowledge of ingredients and spices. We still shop together at various markets and spice stores and are constantly inspired by their exotic colors and aromas.

We hope you will see and taste many flavors of the world using the recipes in this collection. So tie on your apron and prepare for thrills ahead!

Bill Lombardo and Thach Bui
Toronto, February 1995

Cheap Thrills Cuisine®

with Chef Peppi

Chef Peppi

Breakfast Specialties

Mother's Day Muffins

In a large bowl, mix:
1½ cups bran
1 cup sifted flour
1 tsp baking powder
½ tsp baking soda
¼ tsp salt
¼ cup brown sugar
¼ cup raisins
Heat until hot:
1 cup milk
¼ cup molasses
¼ cup soft butter
Remove from heat...
...and blend into mix with a spatula.
Beat one egg for 2 min. Stir it into wet mix.
Scoop into muffin cups.
Icecream scoop
Bake in 400°F oven for 20-25 min. or until center is spongy. Makes 10 to 12 muffins.

Cheap Thrills Cuisine®
with Chef Peppi

Parisian French Toast

Remove a 1-inch center from two 3/4-inch thick slices of French bread.

Dip each slice on both sides in 2 well-beaten eggs seasoned with 1/4 tsp of cinnamon and a dash of salt and pepper.

Fry in 1 Tbsp butter on a gentle heat.
Chef Peppi

Break a medium egg into each center and allow to firm. (1 minute)

When bread is golden brown, flip over and...
color opposite side on slightly higher heat.
MAPLE SYRUP

Serves 2 with hot maple syrup or preserves.

Breakfast Specialties

Grapefruit Warm-Ups

Great as a menu starter or a break-fast pick-you-up.
Preheat your oven to 350°F.
Slice a large grapefruit in half.
Cut around each section freeing flesh from the core.
Place grapefruit halves in an ovenproof dish.
Sprinkle with:
1 Tbsp Demerara or brown sugar
1 tsp pure vanilla extract
Bake for 25 min,
Grapefruit will get very tender and juices will spill over.
Spoon pan juices on top.
Serves two in high-sided bowls.

Cheap Thrills Cuisine®
with Chef Peppi

Easter Shirred Eggs

Preheat oven to 400°F. Melt 1 tsp butter in an 8" nonstick or glass ovenproof dish.
Carefully break 2 eggs into dish.
Keep yolks intact.
Place thinly sliced onion, mushroom and cooked ham on egg whites only.
Heat 1 Tbsp butter to bubbling.
Pour over egg whites and sprinkle with paprika.
Bake for 8 to 10 min. or until egg whites are firm, with yolks staying soft.
Serve hot with toast.

Breakfast Specialties

Breakfast Tips

Tired of broken egg yolks and burnt, greasy bacon? Here are some helpful hints.

To save on clean-up, cook ham, sausage or bacon in 350°F oven for 15-25 minutes.

Place food on foil-lined tray & turn over once.

To poach an egg.

Break egg into a small cup and slip into simmering water.

5 parts H_2O
1 part vinegar
Cook for 3 minutes.

Egg will congeal & lift out whole.

Easy-over egg without flipping.

When one side is done, add 1 Tbsp of water.

Cover tightly and cook on low until egg white congeals.

Cheap Thrills Cuisine®
with Chef Peppi

Canadian Breakfast

On medium, sauté two slices of Canadian bacon to a crispy brown.
Arrange on two slices of toasted, buttered English muffin.
Keep warm.

Break 2 eggs into separate cups.
Slip eggs into 2 cups boiling water & 1/4 cup vinegar.
Simmer for 1-2 minutes
until eggs begin to float.
Place on top of bacon & muffin.

Heat & stir 3Tbsp heavy cream until it reduces by half.
Remove from heat.
Blend in 2tsp maple syrup.

Return to medium high and heat to bubbling.
Cool slightly & spoon over eggs.
Serves 1.

Soups

Apple Curry Bisque

Peel, core & dice two large cooking apples.
Sauté in a nonstick pot on medium with 1/2 cup minced onion until tender.
Add:
1 tsp curry powder
1/4 tsp nutmeg
1 cup chicken stock
1/2 cup apple juice
Simmer for 10 min.
Remove from heat and cool 5 minutes.
Purée until smooth!
Blend in 1/2 cup of heavy cream.
Refrigerate 1 hr.
Adjust seasoning with curry & salt.
Sprinkle with grated apple & ground cinnamon.
Serves 4.

Cheap Thrills Cuisine®
with Chef Peppi

Potato, Leek & Broccoli Bisque

6"
Cut, trim and wash 4 med. leek bottoms.
Dice leeks to make about 2 cups.
Sauté in 2 Tbsp butter with 1 med. diced onion.
Add 5 cups of chicken stock.
Bring to a simmer, then add 4 medium peeled, diced potatoes.
Add one bay leaf.
Simmer for 30 min.
Remove bay leaf. Purée on pulse in 3 batches
Return to low simmer.
Blend in 2/3 cup of heavy cream. Add 1/2 cup of blanched broccoli florets.
Heat through & serve warm with multi-grain loaf.
Chef Peppi
Serves 4 in bowls.

Soups

Broccoli Chestnut Bisque

Slit ½ lb of chestnuts.
Roast in 350°F oven for 5 minutes.
Peel and set aside.
In a 3quart pot, sauté on low in 2 Tbsp butter for 10 minutes:
1 tsp minced garlic
½ cup diced onion
1 cup trimmed diced broccoli stems

Stir in 3 Tbsp flour, then add 5 cups chicken stock.
Whisk to a smooth consistency.

Purée half of roasted chestnuts, then add to soup.
Bring to a boil, then add 2 cups broccoli florets. Season with 1 tsp salt.

Simmer for 15 min.
Add ½ cup heavy cream & simmer 2 minutes more.
Serve warm, topped with remaining roasted, chopped chestnuts.
Serves 4

Cheap Thrills Cuisine®
with Chef Peppi

Mulligatawny Soup

Sauté ½ cup each of diced onion, celery, carrot and apple for 2 min. in 2 Tbsp olive oil.
Season with:
1 Tbsp curry powder
½ tsp cumin
½ tsp coriander
½ tsp minced garlic
Dust with 3Tbsp flour.
Blend in well.
Chef Peppi
In 2 stages, whisk in 2 qts. of strong chicken stock to...
...a smooth consistency.
Simmer on low for 5 minutes.
Add 2/3 cup of rice and 1 cup diced chicken.
Cook covered on low for 30-35 min.
Or until rice is tender.
Adjust salt & pepper.
Serves 6-8 with pita bread.

Soups

A Soup for all Seasons

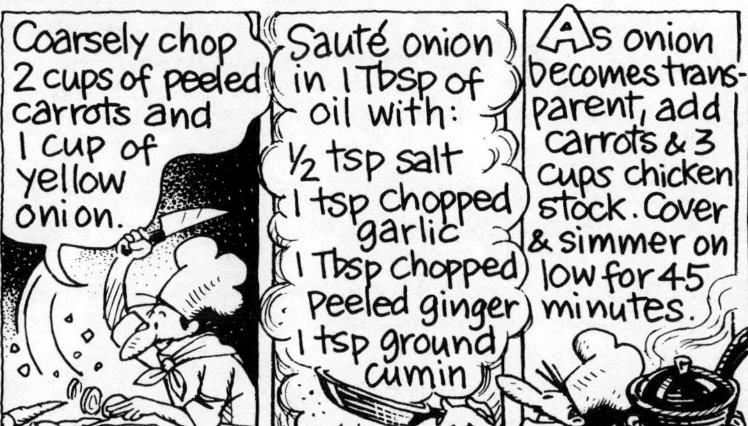
Coarsely chop 2 cups of peeled carrots and 1 cup of yellow onion.
Sauté onion in 1 Tbsp of oil with:
½ tsp salt
1 tsp chopped garlic
1 Tbsp chopped peeled ginger
1 tsp ground cumin
As onion becomes trans-parent, add carrots & 3 cups chicken stock. Cover & simmer on low for 45 minutes.

When carrots break up to touch of a fork...
Process mixture in 2 to 3 stages to a creamy purée.
Stir in ½ cup heavy cream.
Heat to a slow simmer.
Serves 2 with a dollop of sour cream, 1 Tbsp grated carrot and black pepper.

Cheap Thrills Cuisine®
with Chef Peppi

Vegetable Lasagna

1/2 green pepper
1 red pepper
2 celery stalks
2 zucchini
1 onion
Add
6 large diced tomatoes
2 Tbsp tomato paste
1/4 cup each of chopped fresh basil & oregano
1 Tbsp minced garlic
1 tsp salt
Sauté vegetables in 1 Tbsp oil and then add rest of ingredients.
Simmer 15 min. to thicken.
Build lasagna in 4qt. casserole:
2 cups shredded mozzarella
Remainder of tomato sauce
Blanched lasagna
2 Tbsp grated Parmesan
3 cups sliced mushrooms
1 cup crumbled feta or ricotta cheese
10 oz. steamed spinach
Blanched lasagna
1/2 of tomato sauce
1 cup shredded mozzarella
Blanched lasagna
Sprinkle with crushed black peppercorn. Bake in 325° F oven for 45-60 min.
Cool 10 min.
Serves 8-10.

Vegetarian

Chili Non Con Carne

Soak 1 cup each of white, brown and red kidney beans in 2-3 cups of water.

For four hours.

In a 4qt. pot, Sauté 2 cups of diced onions in 3 Tbsp oil.

Season with:
1 Tbsp chili powder
1 Tbsp minced garlic
1 tsp each of cumin & coriander

Add drained beans and 6 cups of water. Simmer covered for 1 hour.

Blend in: 4 cups diced tomatoes
5 Tbsp tomato paste

Add 2 cups each of diced red pepper, celery, zucchini & mushrooms.

Simmer on low for 1 hr.

Season chili with 2 Tbsp each of chopped fresh oregano & cilantro & 1-2 tsp salt.

Optional: 1 or 2 chopped fresh jalapeños

Cook until chili is thick and beans are tender (1/2-1 hour).

Serves 12-15.

Cheap Thrills Cuisine®
with Chef Peppi

Sweet Potato Casserole

Bake in a covered casserole in a 350°F oven for 50 min.
4 medium sweet potatoes
4 med. peeled diced onions
1 medium diced carrot
1/2 cup water
Cool. Cut potatoes & peel by squeezing pulp out of skin.
Mash in a large bowl.
Plop!
Purée onions & carrot in cooking liquid and fold into potatoes.
Mix in 3 large eggs and beat until smooth.
Season with:
1/2 tsp curry
1/2 tsp salt
1/4 tsp pepper
2 Tbsp fresh chopped parsley
Bake in 1 quart covered casserole at 350°F for 50 minutes.
Then Sprinkle with cooked peas.
Serves 8.

Vegetarian

Vegetarian Pasta Shells

Cook 12 large pasta shells in boiling water for 10 minutes.
Rinse in cold water & set aside.
Chef Peppi
Sauté in 2 Tbsp olive oil:
1 tsp minced garlic
1/4 cup each of diced mushrooms, onion, zucchini & red pepper.
Season with 1 tsp ground nutmeg & 1 Tbsp grated Parmesan.
Cool and stir in 2 cups cooked, chopped spinach and one beaten egg.
Blend in 4 Tbsp ricotta cheese. Stuff shells.
Arrange shells on a bed of spicy tomato sauce. Cover and bake in 350°F oven for 10 min.
Top with shredded mozzarella and bake 5 min. longer.
Serve 3 shells with sauce per person.

Cheap Thrills Cuisine®
with Chef Peppi

Razamataz Ratatouille

Sauté on medium in 4 Tbsp olive oil ½-inch dices of:

2 celery stalks
2 med. green peppers
1 large red pepper
4 med. green zucchini
2 med. red onions

Presoak 2 cups of diced eggplant in 1 cup of milk for 1 hour. Strain. Add eggplant and one 28oz. can of diced plum tomatoes to pan.

Season with:

1½ tsp basil
1 tsp oregano
2 tsp minced garlic
2 Tbsp tomato paste
½ tsp salt
½ tsp sugar
1 tsp coarse peppercorn

Simmer 10 min. on medium. Strain veggies.

Then reduce liquid by half.

Add ingredients to 2qt. casserole. Bake uncovered at 350°F for 30 min.

Sprinkle with 2 Tbsp Parmesan cheese & return to oven for 15 min.

Serves 8 with fettuccine.

Vegetarian

Frittata Milanese

Sauté
1 Tbsp minced onion
½ tsp minced garlic
in ½ Tbsp butter for 2 min.
Nonstick ovenproof skillet
Chef Peppi
Preheat oven to 350°F.
Remove from heat and:
Pour in 3 well-beaten eggs.
Arrange thin slices of mushroom around edge and overlap thin slices of tomato in the center.
Sprinkle with 1 tsp fresh chopped oregano.
Bake in 350°F oven for 5 min. Sprinkle with grated Parmesan & black pepper.
Turn heat to 400°F.
Bake 2–3 minutes longer.
Serves 1.

Cheap Thrills Cuisine®
with Chef Peppi

Veggie Kabobs

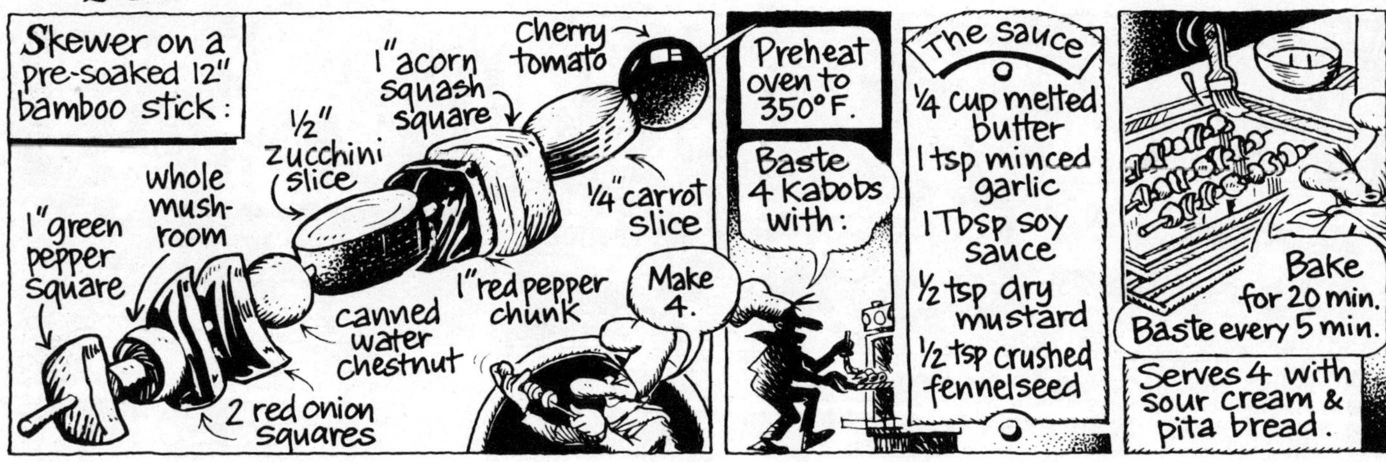
Skewer on a pre-soaked 12" bamboo stick:
1" green pepper square
whole mush-room
2 red onion squares
canned water chestnut
1/2" zucchini slice
1" red pepper chunk
1" acorn squash square
1/4" carrot slice
cherry tomato
Make 4.
Preheat oven to 350°F.
Baste 4 kabobs with:
The sauce
1/4 cup melted butter
1 tsp minced garlic
1 Tbsp soy sauce
1/2 tsp dry mustard
1/2 tsp crushed fennelseed
Bake for 20 min. Baste every 5 min.
Serves 4 with sour cream & pita bread.

Vegetarian

Especially Eggplant

Trim top and cut a medium sized eggplant into 4 1/2" slices.
Salt lightly on both sides.
This method erases the bitter taste.
Patdry, 10 minutes later.
paper towel
Flour both sides.
Fry in 1 Tbsp butter and 1 tsp olive oil, on both sides until golden.
Serves 4.
Try sprinkling with Parmesan cheese or fresh diced garlicky tomatoes.

Cheap Thrills Cuisine®
with Chef Peppi

Greek Salad Sub

Combine and marinate for 30 minutes:
3 diced medium plum tomatoes
1/2 cup diced hothouse cucumber
1/4 cup diced red pepper
2 Tbsp fresh chopped oregano
1/4 tsp salt
2 Tbsp olive oil
1 tsp red wine vinegar
2 tsp minced garlic
Brush sliced baguette (french stick) with olive oil.
Grill until crusty & golden brown.
Toss 2 cups of chopped romaine lettuce with marinated vegetables.
Drain and...
Arrange on toasted baguette.
Sprinkle with 2-3oz. crumbled feta cheese.
Cut baguette in 3 pieces.
Serves 3.

Lamb, Beef & Pork

Lamb Persillé

Tie a 3 to 4 lb de-boned lamb leg and sauté on all sides until brown.
Set aside.
Mix:
2 cups breadcrumbs
1/3 cup chopped parsley
2 tsp minced garlic
1 tsp salt
3 Tbsp melted butter
Coat cooled lamb with 3 Tbsp of Dijon mustard.
Dot with 1 Tbsp crushed peppercorn.
Pat breadcrumb mix on the outside of lamb.
Roast on rack in 350°F oven for 2½ hours.
Cool 10 min. Untie lamb & cut into ½" slices.
Serves 8.

Cheap Thrills Cuisine®
with Chef Peppi

Irish Country Stew

Blanch 2 lbs of diced leg of lamb in 6 cups of boiling water for 15 minutes.

"Skim Vigorously!"

In 8 quart pot, combine lamb and strained broth with:

2 cups diced potato
1 cup each of diced rutabaga, celery, mushroom & onion

Season with:

1 tsp pepper
½ tsp dry rosemary
2 Tbsp fresh chopped dill
1 tsp minced garlic
1 bouillon cube (opt.)
1 bay leaf

For a brown color, add ½ tsp molasses.

Simmer on low for half an hour.

Cook 6 med. peeled cut potatoes for 30 minutes, mash and blend into stew. Simmer 15 min. more.

Serves 6-8.

Sesame Pork Tenderloin

Slice a 12 oz. pork tenderloin into 3 strips.
Section into 1-in. pieces.
Flatten between wax paper to about 3/8-inch thickness.
Marinate, refrigerated, for 8 hours
in:
2 Tbsp oil
2 tsp soy sauce
½ tsp each of minced garlic & fresh ginger
Dash of black pepper

Dip pork scallops in egg, then into 1 cup of sesame seeds spread out on a tray.
2 beaten eggs.

Fry in ½ in. of oil in a large skillet until browned.
Pat dry with paper towel. Serves 4 with spiced rice and hot mustard.

Cheap Thrills Cuisine®
with Chef Peppi

Lamb Chop Mignonette

Marinate overnight in fridge 8 2-oz. loin lamb chops in:
4 Tbsp olive oil
1 Tbsp minced garlic
2 Tbsp fresh chopped basil
1 Tbsp crushed rosemary
4 2-inch pieces each of green pepper & red onion
Skewer lamb chops as shown below...
onion & pepper strips.
6" metal skewers, capped with mushrooms
...with pepper & onion between them.
Press each side into 1 tsp coarse, cracked, black peppercorn.
Preheat BBQ to medium high.
For medium-rare to medium, broil 5 to 7 minutes on each side. Turn once.
Serves 4.

Moroccan Muffuletta

Mince coarsely on pulse Speed: 1/2 cup green olives & 2 Tbsp olive oil.
Mix with: 1 cup each of thin sliced red and green pepper
1 sliced celery stalk
1 tsp sesame seeds
Marinate veggies for 30 min. with:
1/2 tsp thyme
1 tsp garlic
1 tsp basil
1/4 tsp dry mustard
pinch black pepper
1/2 cup olive oil
kaiser roll
1 slice Swiss cheese
2 thin slices of ham
3-4 thin slices of Genoa salami or hot Italian ham
1 slice Swiss cheese
Top with 2 Tbsp of muffuletta mixture
slotted spoon
Serves 1
mint tea

Cheap Thrills Cuisine®
with Chef Peppi

Pepper & Sausage Fettuccine

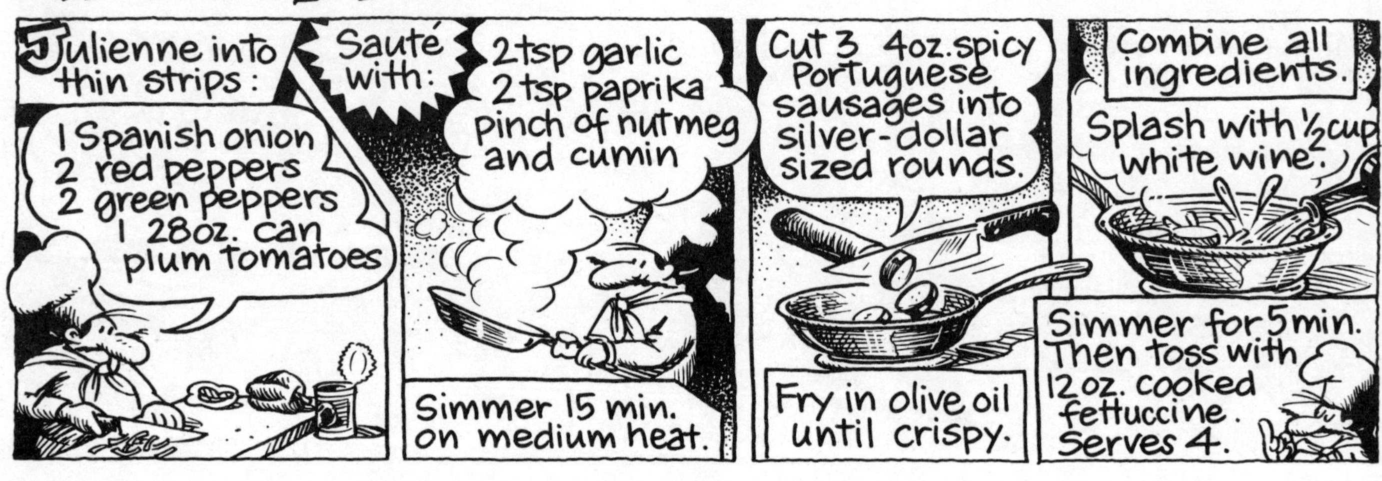
Julienne into thin strips:
1 Spanish onion
2 red peppers
2 green peppers
1 28oz. can plum tomatoes
Sauté with:
2tsp garlic
2 tsp paprika
pinch of nutmeg and cumin
Simmer 15 min. on medium heat.
Cut 3 4oz. spicy Portuguese sausages into silver-dollar sized rounds.
Fry in olive oil until crispy.
Combine all ingredients.
Splash with 1/2 cup white wine.
Simmer for 5 min. Then toss with 12 oz. cooked fettuccine. Serves 4.

Shaker Steak

With a sharp pointed knife or your butcher's help, slit a deep pocket in a 1 to 2 lb flank steak.

(pocket)

Sauté ½ lb of minced pork in 1 Tbsp oil for 2 min.

Add 1 cup each of chopped onion, celery & mushroom.
1 Tbsp basil
½ tsp sage
1 Tbsp minced garlic
2 tsp prepared mustard
½ tsp ground cloves
1 tsp rosemary
2 tsp salt

Blend well.

Mix ingredients in a bowl with 2 cups diced bread & 2 eggs.

Seal end with toothpicks. Sear both sides and...

Braise covered with 1 cup consommé or beef stock for 1½ hrs in 350°F oven

Serves 4-6

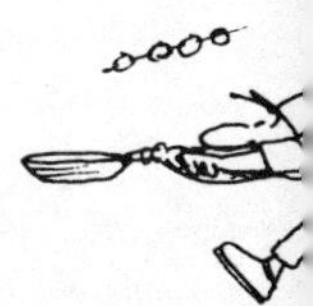

Cheap Thrills Cuisine®
with Chef Peppi

Polynesian Christmas Ham

Prepare this mixture:
1/4 cup prepared mustard
1 cup brown sugar
1/4 tsp ground cloves
1/4 tsp curry
1 Tbsp ground cumin
Using your hands or a ladle, coat a 3-5lb smoked ham with the mixture.
Attach pineapple rings with tooth picks...
rack
2 cups water
Bake in 350°F oven for 30 min.
rack
Remove from oven.
Cover ham with 1-1½ cups pureed mango chutney.
Bake 10 min. or more until chutney crustifies.
Slice ham thinly.
Garnish ham with browned pineapple rings. Serves 10 to 12.

Lamb, Beef & Pork

Osso Buco alla Romana

Flour, salt and pepper four 8 oz. pieces of center cut beef shanks on both sides, patting to make flour stick!

Sauté on medium in 4 Tbsp of olive oil for 5 minutes on each side.

Set aside in a 2 quart casserole dish.

In the same pan sauté ½ inch strips of:

1 med. green pepper
1 med. red pepper
2 med. peeled onions
1 tsp minced garlic
1 tsp oregano
1 tsp dry mustard
1½ tsp basil

When veggies are tender, add one 16 oz. can of tomatoes. Bring to a boil and pour over shanks.

Cover casserole and bake at 350°F for 2½ hrs.

Meat will fall from bones when done. Serves 4-6 with basil-tossed fettuccine.

Cheap Thrills Cuisine®
with Chef Peppi

Oven-Baked Stew

Sear 1½ lbs of ½-inch diced lean top round on high heat in 3 Tbsp oil.

Stir so meat is an even golden dark brown.
ovenproof

Add 1 cup of fine-diced onions and brown as much as possible.

Stir to prevent burning.

Repeat with 2 cups diced mushrooms.

Splash with ½ cup red wine.

Scrape bottom of skillet for meat juices. Dust with 2 Tbsp flour.

Add 1½ cups of very strong stock, blending to a smooth consistency.

Cover skillet and bake in 300°F oven for 55 min. Season with salt & pepper.

Bake uncovered for 10 min. longer.

Serves 4 on noodles.

Pork Thai Noodles

Soak 1 cup cellophane rice noodles for 15 min. in hot water.
Rice Noodle
Drain
Cut into 1" strands.
In a hot wok Stir fry :
1/2 lb of lean pork (thinly sliced)
1 slice ginger
1 crushed clove of garlic
3 Tbsp oil
3 minutes
Add the following to wok:
5 chopped water chestnuts
1 diced red pepper
1 cup shredded spinach
2 Tbsp fermented black beans
2 Tbsp beer
2 Tbsp cornstarch
Stir fry 2-3 minutes.
Toss in noodles at high heat for 2 more minutes.
Garnish with chopped roasted peanuts. Serves 2.

Cheap Thrills Cuisine®
with Chef Peppi

Cajun Stuffed Peppers

Sauté on medium, in 1 Tbsp of vegetable oil, for 5 min.
1/4 cup diced red onion
1/4 cup diced red pepper
1 diced celery stalk
5 oz. diced smoked sausage

Season with:
2 tsp cajun spice
1 tsp crushed fennel seed
1/2 tsp salt

Combine sautéed onion mixture with:
1 cup cooked rice
1 lb lean ground beef
1 beaten egg
1/4 cup corn kernels
1/4 cup bread crumbs

Mix well.

Slice the caps off 6 medium green peppers,

clean them.

Stuff peppers to over flowing.

Mix one 14 oz. can diced tomatoes & 3 Tbsp of salsa sauce in a bowl, then pour over peppers.

casserole

Bake covered at 350°F for 1 hour. Serves 6.

Crusty French Pizza

With a serrated knife slice a French baguette in half lengthwise.

No more than 1" thick.

Spread grated mozzarella or provolone cheese over both slices.

Top with 4oz. canned tomato sauce spiced with 1 tsp each of minced garlic, dry basil & cracked peppercorn.

Finally, add Parmesan cheese, crispy bacon, red onion slices and blanched asparagus spears.

Bake in 450°F oven for 5-10 min. or until cheese is bubbly. Add more grated cheese and...
crustify under broiler.
Serves 6.

Cheap Thrills Cuisine®
with Chef Peppi

Pizza Buttons

Choose 20 large, firm, white mushrooms. Twist off stem gently.
Trim inside to enlarge cavity.
Sauté in 1 Tbsp butter or margarine for 3 minutes:
1 tsp minced garlic
1/2 cup fine-diced onion
2/3 cup fine-diced zucchini
2 Tbsp fresh chopped basil
Remove from heat and blend in 2 Tbsp tomato sauce.
Stuff each mushroom with 1 slice of pepperoni and 1 Tbsp zucchini mix.
Top with shredded mozzarella cheese.
Place mushrooms on parchment paper-lined baking pan. Heat in 350°F oven for 10 min.
Sprinkle with coarse-ground pepper.
Serves 3-5.

Chilaquiles (Mexican Pizza)

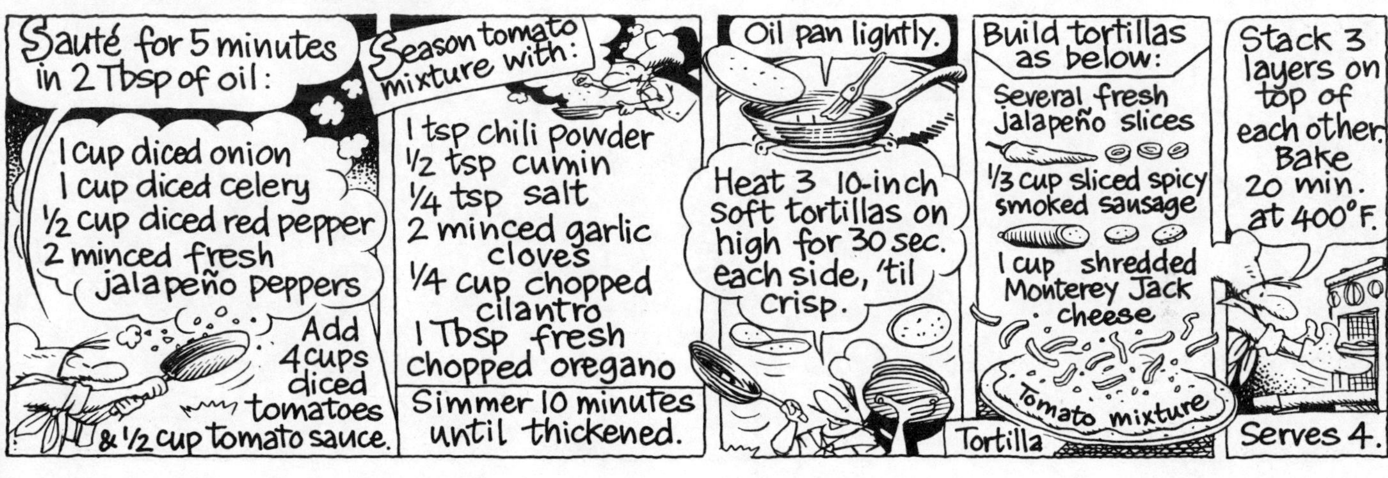
Sauté for 5 minutes in 2 Tbsp of oil:
1 cup diced onion
1 cup diced celery
½ cup diced red pepper
2 minced fresh jalapeño peppers
Add 4 cups diced tomatoes & ½ cup tomato sauce.
Season tomato mixture with:
1 tsp chili powder
½ tsp cumin
¼ tsp salt
2 minced garlic cloves
¼ cup chopped cilantro
1 Tbsp fresh chopped oregano
Simmer 10 minutes until thickened.
Oil pan lightly.
Heat 3 10-inch soft tortillas on high for 30 sec. each side, 'til crisp.
Build tortillas as below:
Several fresh jalapeño slices
⅓ cup sliced spicy smoked sausage
1 cup shredded Monterey Jack cheese
Tomato mixture
Tortilla
Stack 3 layers on top of each other. Bake 20 min. at 400°F.
Serves 4.

Cheap Thrills Cuisine®
with Chef Peppi

Algerian Brochette

Cut 4 4-oz. boneless, skinless chicken breasts into 2" pieces.
About 4-6 pieces per breast.
Marinate in refrigerator for 6hrs. with:
1/4 cup olive oil
2 cups yogurt
2 tsp lemon juice
1 Tbsp chopped fresh oregano
1 Tbsp minced garlic
1 tsp ground cumin
1 Tbsp cracked black peppercorn
Blanch 30 - 1 inch squares of green & red pepper.
boiling water
Arrange chicken & pepper cubes alternately on metal skewers.
Grill on medium B.B.Q. (or 4 inches under broiler) for 8-10 min.
Turn often!
Serves 4
with couscous or lemon rice

Chicken

Vindaloo Chicken

Slice thin & sauté for 5 min. in 2 Tbsp oil:
2 medium onions
1 medium peeled apple

Season with:
1 Tbsp curry powder
1 tsp ground coriander
½ tsp ground cumin
¼ tsp fennel seed
3 cardamom seeds
1 crushed garlic clove
2 thin slices peeled ginger
1 tsp tomato paste
½ tsp salt

Whisk in 2 Tbsp flour & 2 cups of chicken stock.

Simmer 10 min., then transfer to 2 qt. casserole.

Sauté 2 chicken legs in 2 Tbsp oil until browned.

Nestle in curried onions.

Bake covered for 1 hr. in 350°F oven.

And uncovered for 30 more minutes.

Serves 2 on a bed of basmati rice.

Cheap Thrills Cuisine®
with Chef Peppi

Chicken Kiev

Mix 2 Tbsp of soft butter with:
1 Tbsp fine-diced scallion
1 tsp minced garlic
½ Tbsp chopped parsley
¼ tsp salt
Chef Peppi
Flatten two 6oz. boneless, skinless chicken breasts.
basil leaf
half of butter mixture
Fold chicken over.
Seal all sides.
Place chicken in freezer for 30 minutes.
Bread chicken:
flour
2 beaten eggs
bread-crumbs
Deep-fry in hot oil for 3-5 minutes,
or until all sides are brown.
Bake in 325°F oven for 30 minutes.
Serves 2.

Chicken

Chicken Basilico

Sauté on low for 5 min. in 1tsp olive oil:
1/4 cup chopped scallions
1/4 cup zucchini match sticks
2 Tbsp fresh chopped basil
1/2 tsp minced garlic
Cool mixture. Blend in 1/4 cup shredded mozzarella.
Flatten 2 boneless, skinless 4oz. chicken breasts between two sheets of plastic wrap.
Spoon 1/2 of basil mixture on each breast.
Roll up tightly.
Press to seal!
Season with salt & pepper.
Dredge in 1 cup flour.
Sauté in 2 Tbsp hot oil, seam side down.
Brown all sides evenly.
Bake in 350°F oven for 15-20 minutes.
Serve on bed of spaghettini with a chunky style tomato (marinara) sauce.
Serves 2.

Cheap Thrills Cuisine®
with Chef Peppi

New Year's Jumpin' Thai Wings

Purée in a blender on medium speed:
2 stemless jalapeño peppers
1 oz. fresh peeled ginger
1 clove garlic
4 dried chili peppers
1 tsp crushed or ground cardamom
1 tsp curry
1/4 cup coconut oil (available at Asian grocers)
Place mixture in bowl and toss with 1lb chicken wings.
Spread out on a greased baking tray.
Bake wings in preheated 350°F oven for 15-20 min.
Remove and toss in bowl again with 1 Tbsp or more of Tabasco sauce.
Bake for another 10 to 15 min. or until crispy.
Arrange on a bed of steamed rice.
Serves 3-4.
Chef Peppi

Chicken

Thanksgiving Duet

Season inside of 1 1½ lb Cornish hen with ¼ tsp marjoram and ¼ tsp rosemary.
Rub 1 Tbsp oil on skin...
Sprinkle with salt and paprika.
Set hen on rack in a roasting pan.

Sauté on medium in 1 Tbsp butter:

½ cup diced celery & onion
½ cup diced chanterelles or other mushrooms
1 tsp minced garlic
salt & pepper

Add onion mix to 1 cup diced bread. Mix in 1 beaten egg.
Then stuff in hen cavity.

Seal hen with crust of bread.
Bake in 400°F oven for 1-1½ hrs, until golden brown.
Remove crust. Serves 2.

Cheap Thrills Cuisine®
with Chef Peppi

Chicken Pepperonata

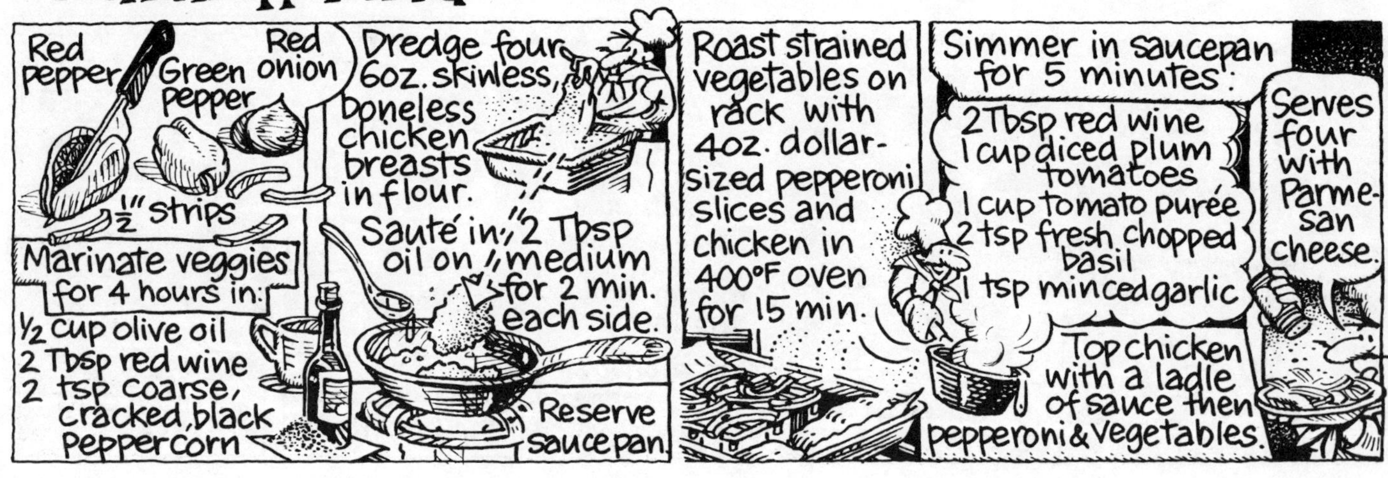
Red pepper
Green pepper
Red onion
1/2" strips
Marinate veggies for 4 hours in:
1/2 cup olive oil
2 Tbsp red wine
2 tsp coarse, cracked, black peppercorn
Dredge four 6oz. skinless, boneless chicken breasts in flour.
Sauté in 2 Tbsp oil on medium for 2 min. each side.
Reserve saucepan.
Roast strained vegetables on rack with 4oz. dollar-sized pepperoni slices and chicken in 400°F oven for 15 min.
Simmer in saucepan for 5 minutes:
2 Tbsp red wine
1 cup diced plum tomatoes
1 cup tomato purée
2 tsp fresh chopped basil
1 tsp minced garlic
Top chicken with a ladle of sauce then pepperoni & vegetables.
Serves four with Parmesan cheese.

Seafood

Coconut Shrimp

Peel, devein & butterfly 6-8 jumbo shrimp.
Sprinkle with a dash of curry & 2 tsp lemon juice.
Mix together:
1 cup bread-crumbs 1/3 cup grated coconut
Beat 3 eggs with 1/4 tsp minced fresh ginger and 1/4 tsp salt.
Dip shrimp in egg...
then into breadcrumb mix.
Coat well.
Heat 2 Tbsp oil & 1 Tbsp butter in a large skillet.
Chef Peppi
Sauté shrimp for 3-5 minutes.
Turn shrimp to brown evenly.
Serves 2 with this dip:
6 Tbsp marmalade
1 Tbsp horseradish
A dash of Worcestershire
(mixed together)
Chef Peppi

Cheap Thrills Cuisine®
with Chef Peppi

Sweet & Sour Shrimp

Marinate 12 cooked jumbo shrimp in:
1 cup vegetable oil
1/2 cup balsamic vinegar
1 Tbsp dry mustard
Refrigerate overnight.

Prepare the following:
pitted, peeled avocado
1/2 in. wedge
lemon
peeled, sectioned grapefruit
Sliced hothouse cucumber
Layer shrimp in center and ladle marinade over.
Serves 2.

Seafood

Sizzling Salmon

Flavor one ½-inch 4 oz. Salmon fillet with:
2 tsp lemon juice
1 tsp olive oil
¼ tsp crushed fennel seed
Refrigerate for 2 hours.

Brush a clean B.B.Q. grill with oil and heat to med. high for 10 minutes.

Brush flesh side of fillet with 1 tsp oil.
Lay fillet on grill diagonally, skin side up. Sear for 3 min.
Lift off carefully. Turn 90° to create pattern. Grill 2 minutes longer.
Season with salt & fresh-ground pepper.
Flip over and grill skin side for 2 min.
Serves 1 with lemon wedges.

Cheap Thrills Cuisine®
with Chef Peppi

B.B.Q. Shrimp "Eyes"

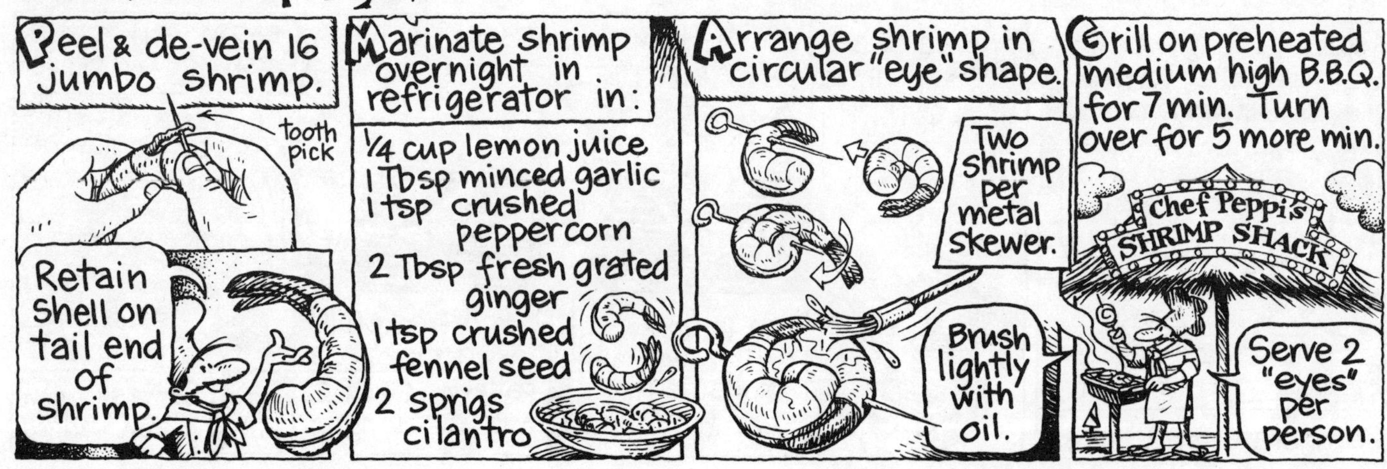
Peel & de-vein 16 jumbo shrimp.
tooth pick
Retain shell on tail end of shrimp.
Marinate shrimp overnight in refrigerator in:
1/4 cup lemon juice
1 Tbsp minced garlic
1 tsp crushed peppercorn
2 Tbsp fresh grated ginger
1 tsp crushed fennel seed
2 sprigs cilantro
Arrange shrimp in circular "eye" shape.
Two shrimp per metal skewer.
Brush lightly with oil.
Grill on preheated medium high B.B.Q. for 7 min. Turn over for 5 more min.
Chef Peppi's SHRIMP SHACK
Serve 2 "eyes" per person.

Seafood

Trout en Papillote

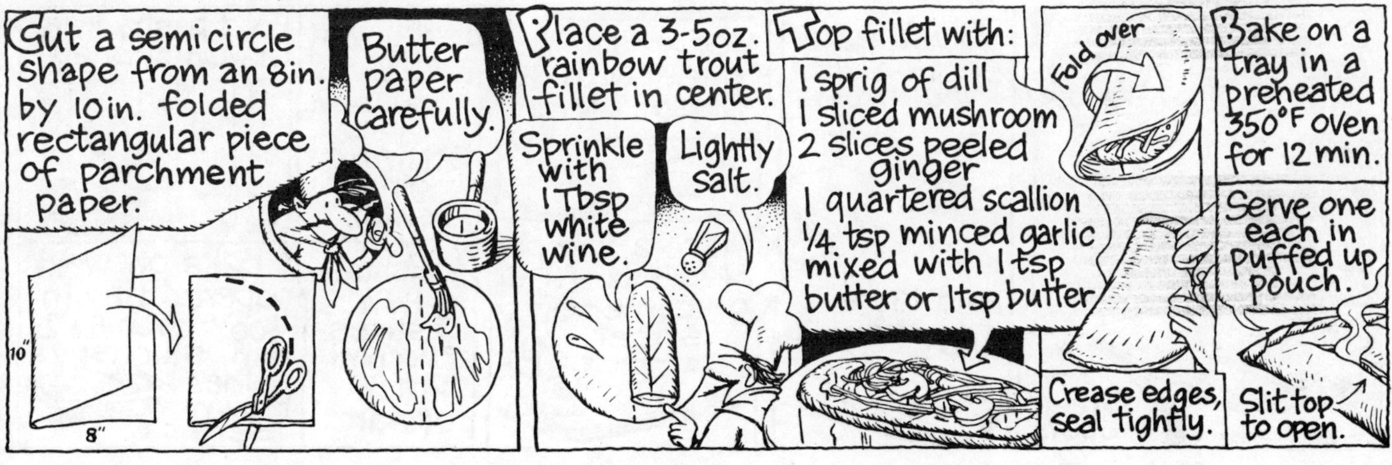
Cut a semi circle shape from an 8in. by 10in. folded rectangular piece of parchment paper.
10"
8"
Butter paper carefully.
Place a 3-5oz. rainbow trout fillet in center.
Sprinkle with 1Tbsp white wine.
Lightly salt.
Top fillet with:
1 sprig of dill
1 sliced mushroom
2 slices peeled ginger
1 quartered scallion
1/4 tsp minced garlic mixed with 1 tsp butter or 1tsp butter
Fold over
Crease edges, seal tightly.
Bake on a tray in a preheated 350°F oven for 12 min.
Serve one each in puffed up pouch.
Slit top to open.

Cheap Thrills Cuisine®
with Chef Peppi

Fresh Salmon Phyllo Puff

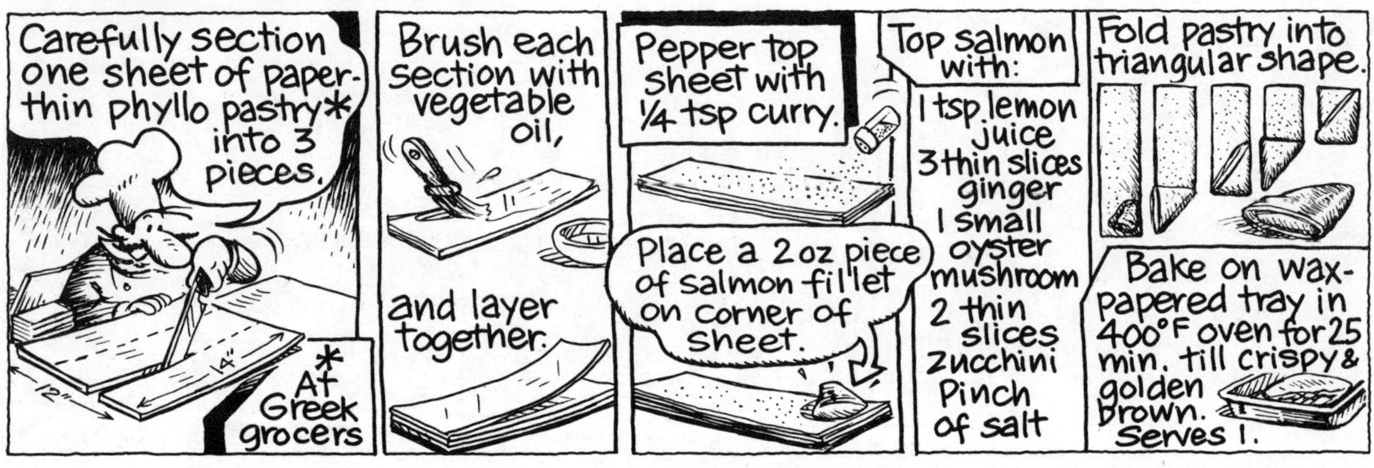
Carefully section one sheet of paper-thin phyllo pastry* into 3 pieces.
14"
12"
* At Greek grocers
Brush each section with vegetable oil,
and layer together.
Pepper top sheet with 1/4 tsp curry.
Place a 2 oz piece of salmon fillet on corner of sheet.
Top salmon with:
1 tsp. lemon juice
3 thin slices ginger
1 small oyster mushroom
2 thin slices zucchini
Pinch of salt
Fold pastry into triangular shape.
Bake on wax-papered tray in 400°F oven for 25 min. till crispy & golden brown. Serves 1.

Sole Belle Meunière

Dip two 4-ounce boneless, skinless sole fillets in mixture of ½ cup milk and 1 beaten egg.
Coat both sides in flour.
On medium heat, sauté each side in:
1 Tbsp hot butter 1 tsp oil
About 1½ min. each side.
Remove sole & keep warm.
Add:
¼ cup thin-sliced mushrooms
3 Tbsp diced fresh tomatoes
Dash of salt & pepper
Sauté on med. high until tender.
Add:
1 tsp lemon juice & a splash white wine
Boil off liquid and spoon sauce over sole.
Sprinkle 1 Tbsp chopped parsley.
Serves 2.

Cheap Thrills Cuisine®
with Chef Peppi

Grilled Bluefish

Boil this marinade and cool it at room temperature.
½ cup lemon juice
¼ cup white wine
1 tsp thyme
1 bay leaf
In a plastic bag, place two 6oz bluefish fillets.
Marinate one hour refrigerated.
Now prepare a basting sauce.

1 cup orange juice
1 tsp minced ginger
3 Tbsp melted butter
1 Tbsp grated orange rind

Arrange fillets on wire rack. Baste with ½ of basting sauce.
Broil for 5 min.
Spread on top:
2 orange slices
1 tsp chopped mint
3-4 red onion rings

...and 1 Tbsp honey. Broil 8 min. more or until flaky. Baste with sauce again.
Serves 2.

SALADS

Japanese Salad

Wash 10oz. bean sprouts under cold running water and drain.

Cut 1 carrot and 3 green peppers into thin strips.

Cook carrot in boiling water for 1 minute.

Add sprouts and pepper.

Turn off heat.

Rinse veggies under cold water.

Drain well.

Mix together in a glass bowl:

1 Tbsp soy sauce
1 tsp rice or cider vinegar
1 Tbsp veg. oil
1 tsp sesame oil

Just before serving, toss in vegetables. Mix well with a pinch of toasted sesame seeds. Serves 4.

Cheap Thrills Cuisine®
with Chef Peppi

Orange Mint Salad

Set aside at room temperature:
Dressing
2/3 cup olive oil
1 tsp lemon juice
1 tsp orange juice
2 tsp white wine
2 tsp chopped fresh mint
Use 6 juicy large oranges.
Cut into 4 or 5 slices.
1/2" thick
Arrange 3 overlapping slices on a bed of radicchio*
Add pepper to taste.
* or leaf lettuce
Drizzle 1 Tbsp of dressing over each serving.
Garnish plates with sliced strawberries and a mint sprig.
Serves 8.

SALADS

Grecian Summer Salad

Combine: 2 cups of ½" diced beefsteak tomatoes with one ½" diced hothouse cucumber.

Make the following marinade of:

½ cup olive oil
1 Tbsp lemon juice
1½ Tbsp red wine vinegar
1 tsp minced garlic
3 Tbsp fresh chopped oregano
1 Tbsp fresh chopped basil
1 tsp salt

Mix together & refrigerate for 4 hours.

Transfer slightly drained salad to 2 qt. bowl lined with Boston lettuce.
Top with ½ cup of crumbled feta cheese.
Serves 4.

Cheap Thrills Cuisine®
with Chef Peppi

Marinated Artichokes

Open two 14oz. Cans of water-packed arti-choke hearts.

Dice into 1/2" chunks.
Save juice.

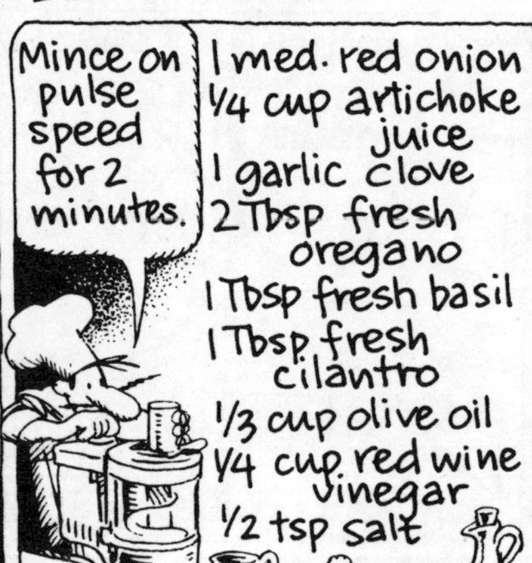

Mince on pulse speed for 2 minutes.
1 med. red onion
1/4 cup artichoke juice
1 garlic clove
2 Tbsp fresh oregano
1 Tbsp fresh basil
1 Tbsp fresh cilantro
1/3 cup olive oil
1/4 cup red wine vinegar
1/2 tsp salt

In a large bowl mix:
1/2 cup each matchstick-thin red & yellow pepper slices
Add chopped arti-choke hearts.

Toss with red onion marinade and refrigerate 1 hour.
Serve on shredded romaine lettuce, garnished with parsley & slices of cucumber & tomato.
Serves 4-6.

SALADS

Bavarian Potato Salad

Sauté 4 slices of bacon until crispy.
Cool & crumble to make bacon bits.
Chef Peppi
Cover 4lb of half-inch diced red potatoes with water & simmer for 5 min. Drain & cool.
Sauté in 1 Tbsp butter for 5 min.:
2 diced medium red onions
2 diced celery stalks
Mix potatoes in large bowl with:
Sautéed onion mix
2 Tbsp. red wine vinegar
2 Tbsp fresh chopped oregano
2 tsp Dijon mustard
1 tsp salt
1 cup mayonnaise
Sprinkle salad with bacon bits and sliced, black pitted olives.
Serves 8-10.

Cheap Thrills Cuisine®
with Chef Peppi

Rosemary Roast Potatoes

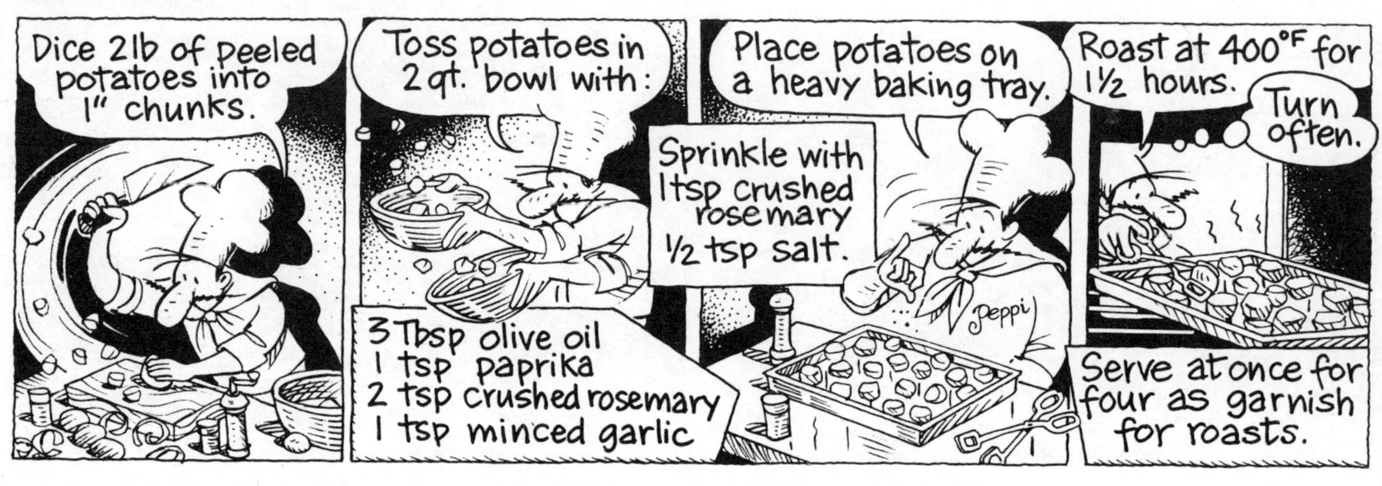
Dice 2lb of peeled potatoes into 1" chunks.
Toss potatoes in 2qt. bowl with:
3 Tbsp olive oil
1 tsp paprika
2 tsp crushed rosemary
1 tsp minced garlic
Place potatoes on a heavy baking tray.
Sprinkle with 1tsp crushed rosemary
1/2 tsp salt.
Peppi
Roast at 400°F for 1 1/2 hours.
Turn often.
Serve at once for four as garnish for roasts.

Side Dishes

Caribbean Rice

Soak 1 cup pigeon peas* for 6 hrs. in 2 cups of water.
*or kidney beans.
In 4qt. pan, sauté 2 Tbsp minced onion in 1 Tbsp butter.
Add drained peas.
Cover with 3 cups of water and 1½ cups of coconut milk.
Stir in:
2 tsp minced garlic
1 Tbsp chopped Scotch bonnet or hot pepper
Simmer on low for 1½ hrs.
Add 2 cups of rice. Bring to boil and simmer for 40 minutes longer or until rice is tender.
Remove from heat and rest for 5 min.
Season with salt & pepper.
Chef Peppi
Serves 8-10.

Cheap Thrills Cuisine®
with Chef Peppi

Baked Onion Pomodoro

Trim and peel 4 2-inch-round cooking onions.
Flat top and bottom
Scoop out center, about 1/3. Brush with oil.

Sauté in 1 Tbsp of olive oil for 2–3 minutes:
1/4 cup diced tomatoes
2 Tbsp fine-diced leek
1/4 tsp minced garlic
1/4 tsp chopped fresh oregano
1/2 Tbsp raisins

Stuff onion with 1–2 Tbsp of tomato mixture.
Sprinkle with salt & pepper. Place in a casserole.

Add 2 Tbsp of water.
Bake covered in 350°F oven for 20 min.

Uncover and bake 10 min. longer.
Cool slightly and serve 1 per person.

Side Dishes

Green Beans & Garlic

Trim, wash and blanch 3/4 lb of green beans in 3 cups of boiling water seasoned with 1/2 tsp salt for 3-5 minutes.

Refresh in cold water.
Set aside.

Heat 1 Tbsp butter on medium high.
Add:
3 Tbsp of fresh chopped tomatoes
1 tsp minced garlic
Stir-fry for 90 sec.

Add beans to skillet & toss with garlic & tomatoes.

Heat through until beans are hot but still crunchy.

Season with fresh-ground black pepper.
Serves 4-6.

Cheap Thrills Cuisine®
with Chef Peppi

Enchanted Endive

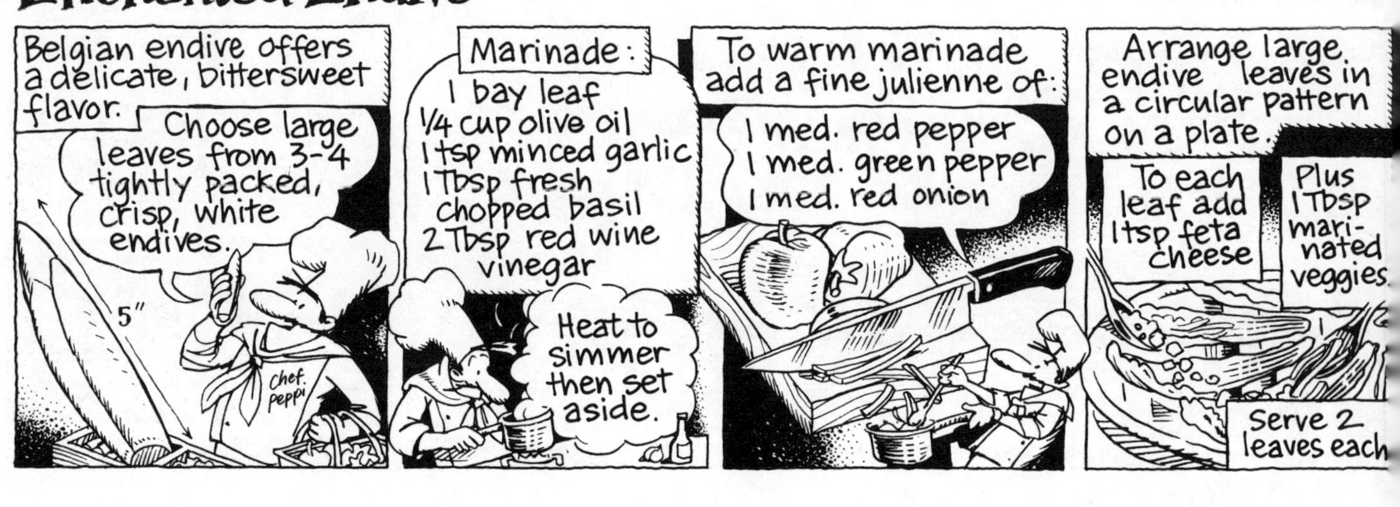
Belgian endive offers a delicate, bittersweet flavor.
Choose large leaves from 3-4 tightly packed, crisp, white endives.
5"
Chef. Peppi
Marinade:
1 bay leaf
1/4 cup olive oil
1 tsp minced garlic
1 Tbsp fresh chopped basil
2 Tbsp red wine vinegar
Heat to simmer then set aside.
To warm marinade add a fine julienne of:
1 med. red pepper
1 med. green pepper
1 med. red onion
Arrange large endive leaves in a circular pattern on a plate.
To each leaf add 1 tsp feta cheese
Plus 1 Tbsp mari-nated veggies.
Serve 2 leaves each

Side Dishes

Stewed Creole Tomatoes

Score an X
on top of 8 plum tomatoes.
Core the bottom & plunge into boiling water for 30 sec.
Refresh in very cold water
and
Slip off the skin.
Cut in half & add to:
2 cups of tomato juice
1 Tbsp tomato paste
2 qt. Pot
Blend in
2 Tbsp chopped fresh basil
1 Tbsp chopped fresh cilantro
1 tsp minced garlic
1/2 cup each of 1/2-in. diced onion, red & green pepper
1 tsp salt
1 tsp sugar
2 dashes Tabasco
1 minced jalapeño (optional)
Bring to boil & reduce heat to medium.
Cover & stew 15 min.
Serves 8.

Cheap Thrills Cuisine®
with Chef Peppi

Herb Glazed Carrots

Cut 4 large peeled carrots into sticks (1½ in. x 3/8 in.).
About 3 cups.
2qt. pot
Add 2/3 cup water. Bring to a boil then add:
1 Tbsp butter 2 tsp sugar
Lower heat, cover & simmer 6 min.
Add: 1 Tbsp each of chopped fresh basil & oregano.
Add 2 Tbsp water. Cover & simmer 2 min. more.
Chef Peppi
Uncover, continue to simmer until all liquid is absorbed or evaporated.
Season with salt & pepper.
Serves 4.

Side Dishes

Broccoli Polonaise

Sauté in 4 Tbsp butter or margarine until tender:

1 minced garlic clove
1 Tbsp fine-diced red onion
2 Tbsp chopped fresh parsley or cilantro

When butter bubbles stir in 1/4 cup breadcrumbs.

Remove from heat and season with dash of salt & 1 tsp lemon juice.

Blanch 4 portions of broccoli tops (12-14 oz.) in boiling water for 5 minutes.

Turn off heat and let sit for two minutes more.

Arrange hot broccoli on plate and spoon 1½ Tbsp warm bread sauce over each portion.

Serves 4 as a vegetable side dish.

Cheap Thrills Cuisine®
with Chef Peppi

Vietnamese Cabbage

Beat 1 egg with 1 tsp fish sauce (or 1½ tsp soy sauce).
Set aside.
Shred ½ lb cabbage leaves into thin strips.
About 2 inches long.
Heat a wok over high flame. Fry 1 crushed garlic clove in 1 Tbsp oil until brown.
Remove it.
Stir fry shredded cabbage for 2 min.
Add 2 Tbsp water. Cook covered at medium heat for 2½ more minutes.
Uncover wok. Turn heat high.
Make a well in cabbage.
Pour in egg-mixture.
Stir fry for 2 more minutes. Season with black pepper. Serves four.

Side Dishes

Crustified Leeks

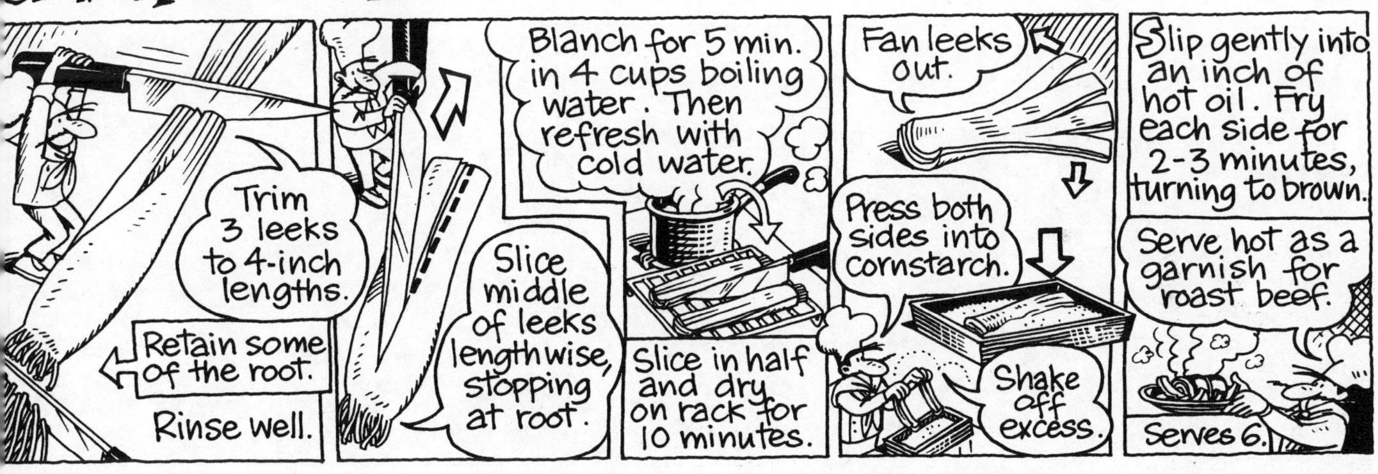
Trim 3 leeks to 4-inch lengths.
Retain some of the root.
Rinse well.
Slice middle of leeks lengthwise, stopping at root.
Blanch for 5 min. in 4 cups boiling water. Then refresh with cold water.
Slice in half and dry on rack for 10 minutes.
Fan leeks out.
Press both sides into cornstarch.
Shake off excess.
Slip gently into an inch of hot oil. Fry each side for 2-3 minutes, turning to brown.
Serve hot as a garnish for roast beef.
Serves 6.

Cheap Thrills Cuisine®
with Chef Peppi

Glazed Cinnamon Squash

Choose a medium-sized acorn squash.
Pick one which is firm and dark green.
Cut squash in half.
Clean out seeds.
Section into 1½ in. pieces.
Boil for 10-15 minutes.
Place on parchment paper-lined sheet pan.
Sprinkle each section with:
1 tsp brown sugar
1/4 tsp ground cinnamon
pinch of nutmeg
Bake at 450°F for 15 min.
Squash should be able to be pricked with a fork.
Serves 6.

Side Dishes

Endive ā la Flamande

Trim ends off 2lb of white endive lettuce. Place in single layer in a buttered casserole dish.
Spear shaped Belgian endive is the best choice.
Add:
4 Tbsp melted butter
2 Tbsp red wine
1 Tbsp sugar
1 Tbsp lemon juice
Bake covered for 30 min. in 400°F oven.
Halfway, turn slightly browned endive over.
Arrange on a warm plate. Sprinkle with Romano cheese.
Serves 4-6.

Cheap Thrills Cuisine®
with Chef Peppi

Saganaki

Slice 8 oz. of feta cheese into 2" x 3/8" squares.
About 8 slices.
Dip cheese slices in mixture of:
1 beaten egg
1 tsp finely chopped fresh oregano
Shake off excess & coat well in flour.
Sauté quickly 4 slices, on medium, in 2 Tbsp olive oil until golden.
Chef Peppi
Remove. Pat dry.
Repeat with other slices.
Season with black pepper. Arrange on plate with thick tomato slices.
Serves 4 with wedges of lemon.

Side Dishes

Eggplant Supremo!

Cut 2 eggplants lengthwise. Wash & salt them lightly.
Rest 10 minutes. Rinse & dry on racks.
Brush skin of eggplants with olive oil.
Bake in preheated 400°F oven for ½ hour.
With skin side down.
Scoop out flesh, leaving a 3/4" wall all around.
Take care not to pierce skin.
Fry the following in 2 Tbsp olive oil for 1 minute:
2 tsp chopped fresh cilantro
1 diced red pepper
1 diced med. onion
1 minced garlic clove
Add eggplant flesh & mix well.
Transfer cooked veggies to eggplant shells.
Alternate with slices of fresh tomato.
Top with ½ lb mozzarella slices.
Bake for 20 minutes longer at 300°F.
Drizzle with 2 tsp olive oil.
Serves 4 as a side dish.

Cheap Thrills Cuisine®
with Chef Peppi

Bruschetta

Prepare the following mixture:
2 medium, 1/4" diced tomatoes
2 Tbsp finely chopped fresh basil
1/2 tsp salt
1/2 tsp minced garlic
1/2 tsp crushed peppercorns

Slice up 1 baguette. (french stick)
1/2" thick
Toast 2" from broiler until golden brown approx. 1 1/2 minutes.

Next rub peeled garlic cloves over each toast.
Brush on extra virgin olive oil.
Top with drained tomato mixture.
Return to 350°F oven for 5 minutes.
Serve with pasta dishes. 2 per person.

SNACKS

Tasty Spring Rolls

Chop:
1 Tbsp shredded peeled ginger
1 Tbsp fresh garlic
Heat in wok in 2 Tbsp oil with 1/2 cup of chopped scallions.
For 30 seconds.

Stir fry for 5 minutes:

2 cups finely sliced bok choy
2 cups shredded carrot
2 cups bean sprouts
2 cups shredded cooked crab or chicken
1/4 cup chopped cilantro

Splash with 2 Tbsp soy sauce & 1 Tbsp lime juice.
Add 1 tsp ground cumin.

Eggwash: Beat 2 eggs with 1 Tbsp water.
Cayenne pepper
Brush on egg wash
①
Spring roll paper (6"x6")
2 Tbsp of mixture
②
③
④
⑤

Fry 4 rolls at a time in 2" hot oil until golden brown.

Drain & keep hot in 200°F oven.

Makes 20.

Cheap Thrills Cuisine®
with Chef Peppi

World Series Nuts

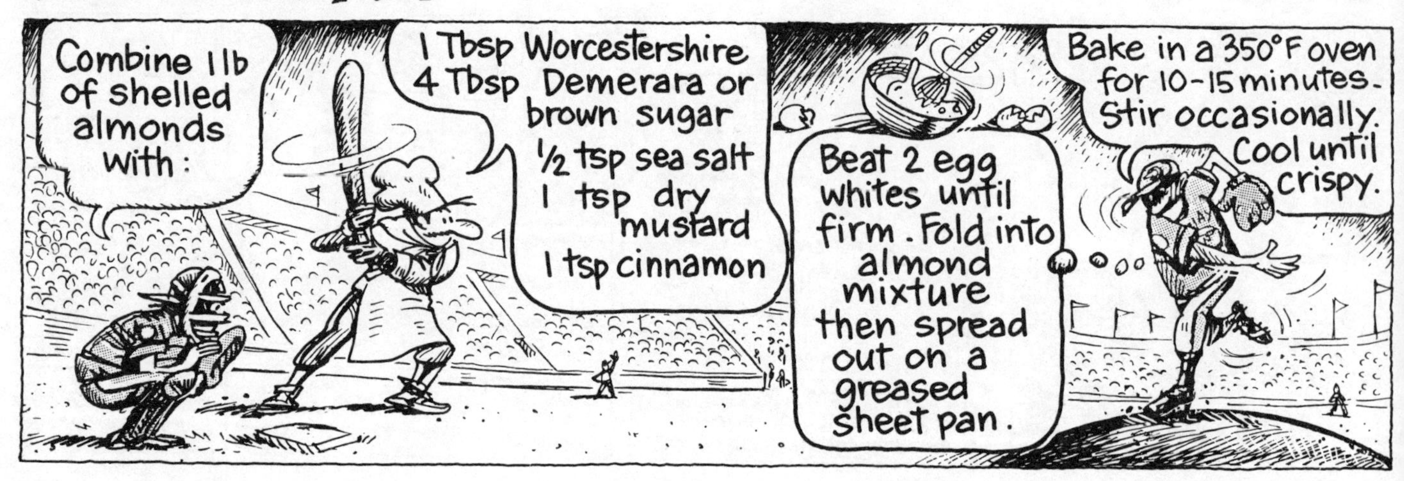
Combine 1 lb of shelled almonds with:
1 Tbsp Worcestershire
4 Tbsp Demerara or brown sugar
1/2 tsp sea salt
1 tsp dry mustard
1 tsp cinnamon
Beat 2 egg whites until firm. Fold into almond mixture then spread out on a greased sheet pan.
Bake in a 350°F oven for 10-15 minutes. Stir occasionally. Cool until crispy.

SNACKS

Quick Cornbread

For spongy, rich corn bread, mix:
3/4 cup corn meal
1/4 cup milk
Let it rest 5 min.

In another bowl combine in following order:

2 beaten eggs
1/4 cup soft butter
1/3 cup maple syrup
1 tsp salt
1 Tbsp baking powder
1 cup sifted flour
1 Tbsp sugar

Knead in corn-meal until it's a lumpy batter.
Greased loaf pan.
3/4 full
Bake in 400°F preheated oven for 35-45 min.
Or until inserted knife shows clean.
Cool 15 min. Turn out. Cut into 1/2 in. slices.

Cheap Thrills Cuisine®
with Chef Peppi

Choco-Nut Chippers

Cream together in 4qt. bowl:
1/2 cup each soft margarine and butter
1/2 cup brown sugar
1 cup white sugar
2 beaten eggs
1 tsp molasses
1 tsp vanilla
2 Tbsp warm water
Sift 2 cups flour with 1 tsp each of baking soda and baking powder.
Mix with spatula into creamed butter in two stages.
Blend in:
2 cups rolled oats
2/3 cup chopped pecans
1/4 cup pine nuts
1/4 cup chopped almonds
1 1/2 cups semi-sweet chocolate chips
Roll dough into small balls.
Press with fork onto greased baking trays.
Bake 8-10 min. in 350°F oven. Cool 5 min. Makes 50 cookies.

Banana Date Loaf

Cream together:
1/2 cup shortening
1 cup sugar
2 well-beaten eggs
2 ripe mashed bananas
Add
1/2 tsp vanilla
1 tsp lemon juice

Sift together:
2 cups flour
3 tsp baking powder
1/2 tsp salt
Mix in 3 stages until sticky dough forms.

Fold in 1/2 cup chopped dates.
Greased loaf pan
2 1/2"
4"
8"
Bake in 375° F oven for 50-60 minutes or until inserted knife comes out clean.

Cool 5 minutes.
Turn out and cool 10 min. longer.
Serves 8-10 slices.

Cheap Thrills Cuisine®
with Chef Peppi

Shortbread Cookies

Cream together 1½ lbs unsalted butter at room temperature with:
1 tsp vanilla extract
½ tsp salt
1½ cups confectioners' sugar
Gradually add:
3 cups flour
2 cups cornstarch
until mixture forms a dough.
Divide it into 5 equal parts.

Roll each on lightly floured board into cylinder shape.
Divide into 1" sections.

Roll dough into ping-pong sized balls. Makes 6 doz. cookies

Press down with a fork.
Garnish with slices of red & green maraschino cherries.
Bake in 350°F oven for 25-30 minutes or until edges turn golden brown. Cool 10 min. and serve.

SNACKS

Ghoul's Drops

Melt 12 oz. of dark semi-sweet chocolate.
Stir constantly until smooth.
steam
double boiler

½ cup rolled oats
½ cup shredded coconut
¼ cup chopped peanuts
2 Tbsp of brandy
Mix this into melted chocolate.

Scoop teaspoonfuls of mixture onto wax paper.
Chill for ½ hour in fridge.
Makes 24 cookies

Cheap Thrills Cuisine®
with Chef Peppi

Humble Hummus

Drain one 19oz. can of chickpeas.
Save the juice!
Purée peas on pulse speed until creamy.
With:
1/4 cup chopped red onion
1/2 cup chickpea juice
2 peeled garlic cloves
Blend in:
1 Tbsp tahini
2 tsp lime juice
1 tsp lime zest
1 tsp cumin
1 tsp nutmeg
4-5 drops Tabasco
Refrigerate in glass or ceramic bowl.
Chef Peppi
Sprinkle with fresh chopped cilantro.
Makes 1-1½ cups of dip for vegetables or tortilla chips.

Sauces & Dips

Asparagus Vinaigrette

Trim 1 lb of asparagus to 4-5 inch lengths. Score bottom of larger stalks.

Blanch asparagus in 1 quart of boiling water for 3-5 minutes.

Drain and refresh with cold running water.

Whisk vigorously:

3 Tbsp olive oil
1 Tbsp red wine vinegar
1 tsp minced garlic
2 Tbsp chopped scallions
1/4 cup matchstick-thin red pepper

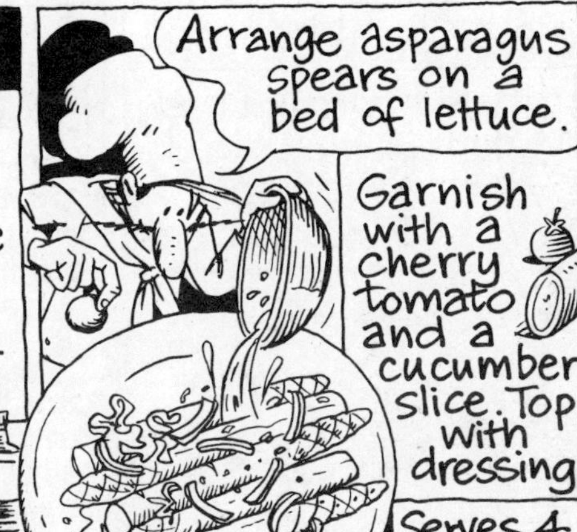
Arrange asparagus spears on a bed of lettuce.
Garnish with a cherry tomato and a cucumber slice. Top with dressing.

Serves 4.

Cheap Thrills Cuisine®
with Chef Peppi

Bolognese Sauce

Sauté until browned:
2lb lean ground beef
1/2 cup each of diced onion & celery
2 minced garlic cloves
Drain fat from meat.
Transfer to 4qt. pot.

Add 2 28oz. cans of plum tomatoes and 2 5½oz. cans of tomato paste.
Simmer on low with 1qt. chicken stock & 1qt. water for 2-2½ hours.

After 1 hour blend in:
3Tbsp basil
1Tbsp oregano
1 tsp crushed peppercorn
1 tsp Salt
1 Tbsp prepared mustard

When sauce is well thickened, adjust seasonings.
Spoon over cooked pasta.

Sprinkle with cooked frozen peas & Parmesan Cheese.
Serves 8.

Sauces & Dips

Hot Cinnamon B.B.Q. Sauce

Cook covered, on low heat, in 1 Tbsp oil for 5 minutes:
1 chopped onion
1 diced garlic clove
1/2 tsp chili powder
1/2 tsp crushed peppercorn
2-3 sprigs cilantro
Purée in food processor with:
1 Tbsp oil
1/4 cup red wine vinegar
1 Tbsp soy sauce
1 tsp tomato paste
And 1 1/2 cups ketchup.
Transfer to sauce pan and mix in:
1 tsp Dijon mustard
1/2 tsp cinnamon
1/2 tsp cumin
1 tsp hot sauce
Heat through then turn off.
Adjust seasoning with hot sauce or cinnamon.
Use as baste for ribs, lamb or chicken!
Chef Peppi
Yields 2 cups.

Cheap Thrills Cuisine®
with Chef Peppi

Chunky Marinara Sauce

Dice into ½-inch chunks:
1 cup red onion
1 cup celery
1 cup zucchini
1 cup mushrooms

Sauté veggies in 2 Tbsp oil for 5 min.
Chef Peppi
Add 4 cups diced, peeled tomatoes. About 8 medium.

Blend in:
1 cup tomato juice
2 Tbsp tomato paste
2 Tbsp fresh chopped basil
1 Tbsp fresh chopped oregano
1 tsp minced garlic
1/4 tsp each sugar, salt & pepper

Simmer on low for 20 minutes or until sauce reduces by 1/3.

Remove from heat and blend in ½ Tbsp finely grated Parmesan.
Serves 6 on top of fresh pasta.

Sauces & Dips

Hurry Curry Dip

Fold 2/3 cup of mayonnaise with 1 cup sour cream.
Chef Peppi
Blend in 1/3 cup apple juice.
Chop 2-3 sprigs of fresh dill very fine.
Add to mix with 1/2 tsp minced garlic.
Chef Peppi
Peel, Core 1 tart apple. Dice in small pieces & stir in.

Season mixture with 1-2 tsp of curry,
1/2 tsp of cumin & a dash of salt.
Serves 6 with raw vege-tables.

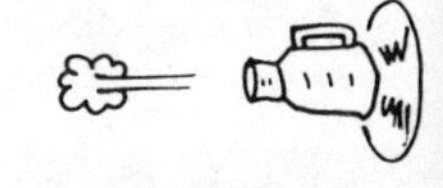

Cheap Thrills Cuisine®
with Chef Peppi

Presto it's Pesto

You'll need a food processor or a blender.
Pick 4 cups of fresh basil leaves.
Put 2 cups of basil in processor with ½ cup of olive oil.
Purée on pulse speed.
Add 6 large peeled garlic cloves and purée again.
Stir in ½ cup of pine nuts. Purée.
Add the remaining basil leaves. Pulse until it forms a runny paste.
Season with 1tsp salt & 1Tbsp of Parmesan cheese.
Recipe makes one cup of spicy pesto sauce.
Try on garlic bread.
Use as a base for cheese pizzas.
Pesto's great as a flavor enhancer for sauces.

Desserts

Apple Rhubarb Crisp

Combine to make a crumble:
1/2 cup melted butter
1 cup graham cracker crumbs
1/4 cup brown sugar
Chef Peppi
Trim 6 rhubarb stalks. Cover with foil and bake for 5 min. in 350°F oven.
Cool & dice in 1-inch chunks.
Combine with 2 peeled, thin-sliced McIntosh apples.
Blend in:
1 cup brown sugar
1/3 cup currants
1 tsp vanilla
1/2 tsp ground nutmeg
Spread 1/2 of crumble in 1qt. casserole.
Add rhubarb & apple mixture, top with remaining crumble. Bake at 350°F for 30 min.
Cool slightly & serve!
Serves 6.

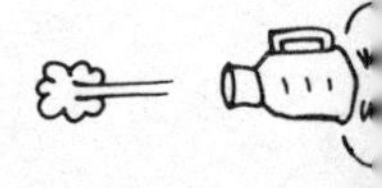

Cheap Thrills Cuisine®
with Chef Peppi

Strudel Surprise

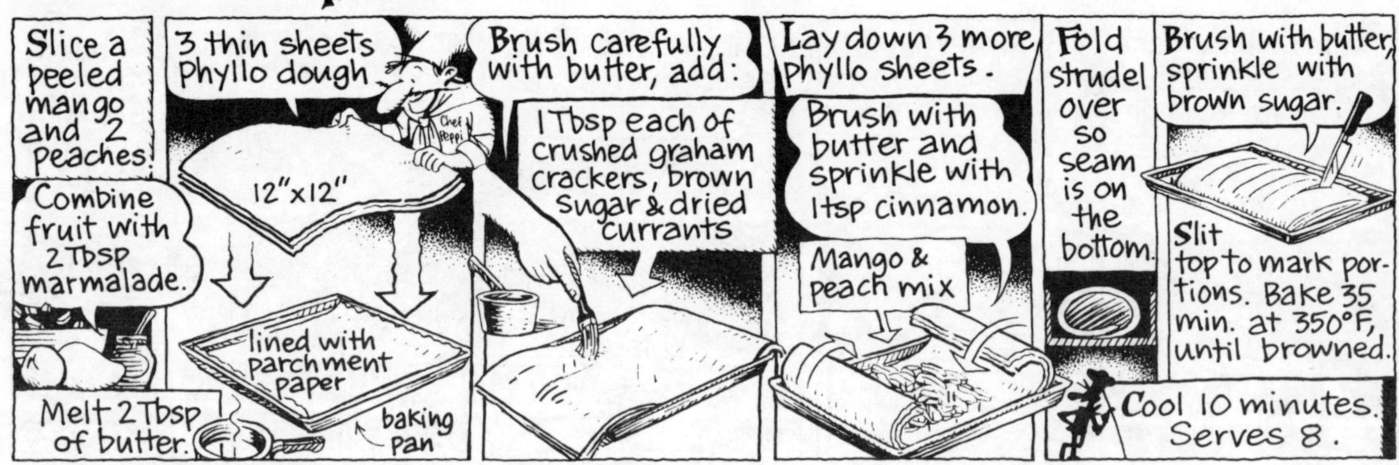
Slice a peeled mango and 2 peaches.
Combine fruit with 2Tbsp marmalade.
Melt 2Tbsp of butter.
3 thin sheets phyllo dough
12"x12"
Chef Peppi
lined with parchment paper
baking pan
Brush carefully with butter, add:
1Tbsp each of crushed graham crackers, brown sugar & dried currants
Lay down 3 more phyllo sheets.
Brush with butter and sprinkle with 1tsp cinnamon.
Mango & peach mix
Fold strudel over so seam is on the bottom.
Brush with butter, sprinkle with brown sugar.
Slit top to mark portions. Bake 35 min. at 350°F, until browned.
Cool 10 minutes. Serves 8.

Desserts

Oktoberfest Apfel

Use aluminum foil to form 4 bags for 4 Cortland apples.

Cut out center core.
Place in bag
Fill apple center with the following mixture:
1 Tbsp brown sugar
1 Tbsp chopped nuts
1/4 tsp cinnamon

350°F oven
Pour in each apple & bag: 1/4 cup of beer. Place on a baking tray.
Bake for 10-12 min.

Serve apples piping hot, still in bags. A great side dish!

Cheap Thrills Cuisine®
with Chef Peppi

Apple Brown Betsy

Slice 4 large, pared, cored, tart apples into 3/8" wedges.
Toss with 2 Tbsp lemon juice.
Keep cool!
Mix: 1/4 cup flour
1 cup brown sugar
1/2 tsp nutmeg
pinch of salt
1/4 cup lukewarm water
Toss with apples and 2 Tbsp currants.
Press into 1 1/2 qt. casserole.
combine:
3 Tbsp melted butter
1/2 tsp cinnamon
1 Tbsp brown sugar
1 tsp vanilla
...with 2 cups of 1/2" cubed raisin bread.
Spread cubed bread over top of apples.
Bake covered in 350°F oven for 45 min.
Then uncovered for 10 more min.
Serve warm for 6, garnished with blueberries & raspberries.

Desserts

Fried Bananas

Peel 10 ripe bananas.
Cover and set aside for 15 min.
Blend together:
1/2 cup rice flour *
1 cup white flour
2 tsp baking powder
1/2 tsp salt
Add slowly until well mixed to:
1 cup cold water
1 large beaten egg
1 cup coconut milk*
*Available in Asian markets.
Heat 1 cup of veg. oil in a wok until smoking. Reduce heat slightly.
Banana
Batter
Slide in carefully.
Cook in batches, three at a time, until golden brown.
Turn over only once. Keep oil hot for a light & crispy finish.
Serve 2 per person with a sprinkle of brown sugar & cinnamon. Top with grated, toasted coconut.

Cheap Thrills Cuisine®
with Chef Peppi

Sweetheart Strawberry Delight

Be my Valentine!
Beat 1 cup whipping cream at medium for 5 minutes.
Peppi
Fold in ½ cup confectioners' sugar.
Add 1 stiffly beaten egg white.
Continue to beat 'til fluffy.
Purée 1 pint fresh strawberries & 3 tsp maraschino cherry juice.
Fold purée in 2 stages into...
...whipped cream mixture.
Dish into 6 chilled wine glasses.
Chill for 30 minutes. Top with a maraschino cherry.
Drizzle each with 1 tsp grenadine.

Desserts

A Trifle Tropical

Slice 3 bananas, 2 mangoes and 1 pineapple in thin 1-inch pieces.
Marinate in 1/4 cup sherry for 2 hours.

Cut an 8"x8"x2" white cake into 3 slabs.
Whip 3 cups heavy cream with 2Tbsp of sugar to stiff peaks.

Sprinkle each cake layer with 2 Tbsp sherry.

Arrange alternating layers of cake, cream & fruit ending with cream on top.

Decorate top with sliced kiwi & strawberries.
cream
fruit
cream
cake
fruit
cream
cake
fruit
cream
cake
Refrigerate overnight.
Before serving, sprinkle with confectioners' sugar.
Serves 12-15.

Cheap Thrills Cuisine®
with Chef Peppi

Bread Pudding

Scald 2 cups of milk with 2 Tbsp sugar and ½ tsp salt (optional).
MILK
Chef! Peppi
Remove from heat &
mix in 1 beaten egg.

Add: 2 Tbsp melted butter and 2 cups of ½-inch diced day-old French baguette.

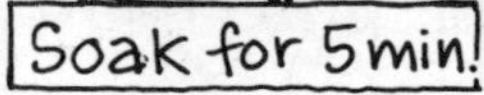

Soak for 5 min.

Mix in:
2 Tbsp currants
2 Tbsp raisins
Ladle pudding mix into a buttered 1 qt. casserole dish placed inside a baking pan.
Sprinkle with cinnamon and nutmeg.
Fill baking pan with ½ inch of water.
Bake in 350°F oven for 1¼ hours.
Serves 6.

Desserts

Tiramisu - "Pick me up"

Filter 2 Tbsp fine-ground coffee * using 1/3 cup of boiling water.
Mix with 3 Tbsp brandy 1/4 cup coffee liqueur
* or 1/4 cup espresso
Cream together for 5 minutes:
1 lb soft mascarpone cheese
6 egg yolks
6 Tbsp sugar
Fold in 6 beaten egg whites
In a separate bowl, whip 1 cup of heavy cream with 2 Tbsp sugar.
Soak 20 lady-fingers in coffee mixture for 5 minutes.
In a 4"x8" casserole dish arrange 2 layers each of:
A. lady-fingers
B. creamed cheese
C. whipped cream
D. shaved chocolate
D
C
B
A
D
C
B
A
Refrigerate 3 hrs. Serves 12.

Cheap Thrills Cuisine®
with Chef Peppi

Chocolate Mousse Cheese Pie

Mix well:
1 1/2 cups graham cracker crumbs
1/2 cup sugar
1 cup melted butter
Press crumb mix into a 9" pie plate with a large spoon.
Cool in fridge.

Cream together:
1/2 lb room temperature cream cheese
4 oz. melted unsweetened chocolate
1/2 cup sugar
Chef Peppi

Prepare a 1 1/2 oz. package of powdered Dream Whip & fold into 1 cup sour cream.
Fold into chocolate mix in 3 stages. Add sugar if needed.
Chilled crust
Smooth with a wet knife, then bake in 350°F oven for 5 min.
Top with crushed toasted almonds. Chill for 2 hours.
Serves 8.

Desserts

Sour Cream Coffee Cake

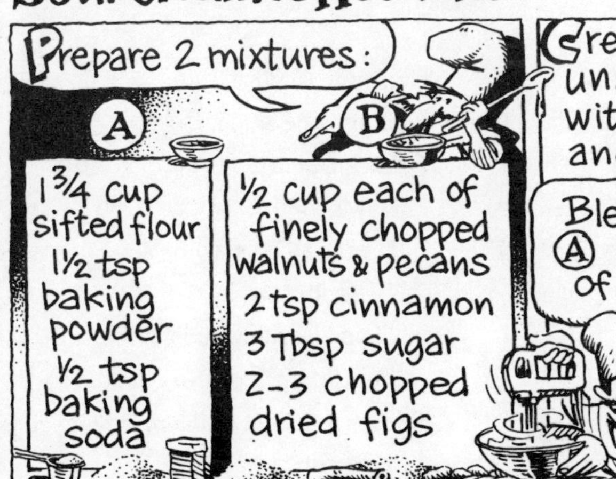
Prepare 2 mixtures:
A
B
1 3/4 cup sifted flour
1 1/2 tsp baking powder
1/2 tsp baking soda
1/2 cup each of finely chopped walnuts & pecans
2 tsp cinnamon
3 Tbsp sugar
2-3 chopped dried figs

Cream 1/2 lb soft unsalted butter with 1 cup sugar and three eggs.

Blend in mixture (A) and 1 1/2 cups of sour cream alternately in two stages.

Swirl in 1/2 of mixture (B) and 1 tsp vanilla.
Pour into a 10-inch diameter buttered Bundt pan.

Top with leftover mixture (B).

Bake in 350°F oven for 1 hr. Cool 10 min., turn out. Serves 10-12.

Index

Index